ROLF OF

Football League champions		FA Cup w		
1900-01	1976-77	1964-6		1975-76
1905-06	1978-79	1973-74		
1921-22	1979-80	1985-86		League/Milk Cup winners
1922-23	1981-82	1988-89		
1946-47	1982-83			1980-81
1963-64	1983-84	European Cup winners		1981-82
1965-66	1985-86			1982-83
1972-73	1987-88	1976-77		1983-84
1975-76	1989-90	1977-78		
		1980-81		
		1983-84		

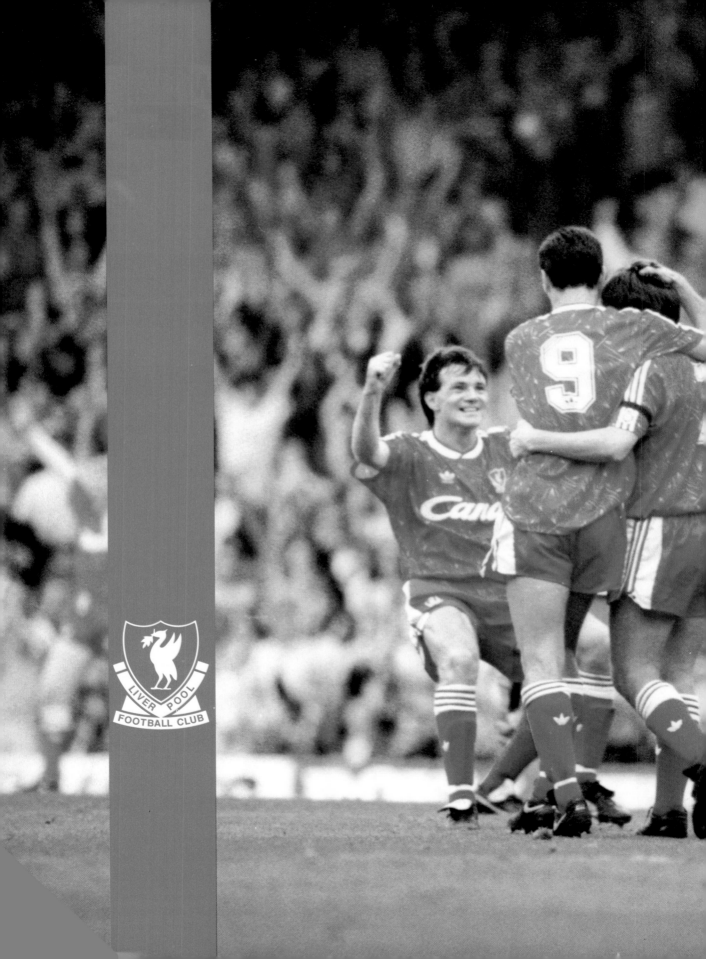

THE OFFICIAL
LIVERPOOL
1992 ANNUAL

STAN LIVERSEDGE

FOREWORD BY IAN RUSH

HAMLYN

CONTENTS

The Man For The Job	7
Foreword by Ian Rush	
Honours Even Charity Shield	8
August Reds Set The Standard	10
September Six Of The Best	12
October The Reds Go Marching On	14
That's A RUSH job!	16
Peter The Great	18
November Rock-Solid	20
December The Pack Closes In	22
Pick of the Pix	24
Ray Houghton Plays The Numbers Game	26
Kenny Hangs Up His Boots	28
Brucie's Clean Sheets	30
January Struggle For Supremacy	32
Demolition Derby	34
February A Roller-Coaster Month	36
Kenny Bows Out	38
Their Cup Runneth Over!	40
Thanks For The Memories	42
Out Of The Frying Pan	44
Quiz	46
Here's To The Next Hundred!	48
March Mixed Fortunes	52
April A New Start?	54
Return Of A Legend	56
May Hopes Are Dashed	58
Back Into Europe	60

Photographic Acknowledgements

Front and back cover: Colorsport
All other photographs are by
John Cocks/Photographique except for the following:
AllSport, 15, 31, 38, ; AllSport/Ben Radford, 6, 7 ;
AllSport/Simon Bruty, 19 ; AllSport/Shaun Botterill, 22,
23 ; AllSport/Dan Smith, 16, 30 ; Harry Ormesher, 31 ;
AllSport/Russell Cheyne 36, 37 ; AllSport/David Cannon, 42,
50, 51, 56, 57.

Published in 1991 by
The Hamlyn Publishing Group Ltd
part of Reed International Books
Michelin House, 81 Fulham Road
London SW3 6RB

© Reed International Books Ltd 1991

ISBN 0 600 57309 5

Printed in Great Britain

The Man for the Job

PEOPLE have often asked me in the past few months whether I felt Graeme Souness was the right man to take over managing Liverpool. The answer is simple: He was the ONLY man for the job.

Even when Graeme was club captain and I was just establishing myself in the team, I felt that he would one day manage this club. It was in his blood already. That's why I was so delighted - and relieved - when he left Rangers to come back to us.

It was just the tonic we needed after all the upheaval caused by the departure of Kenny Dalglish. We wanted someone who knew the Liverpool Way, who would not seek to make wholesale changes to the way the club has been run so successfully over the decades.

But we also needed someone with a tough, ruthless edge. And he certainly fits that bill. You don't muck about with Graeme; he's nobody's fool. He's a very fair man - but a very hard one, as well. If he feels that somebody is not pulling his weight, he'll come down with a heavy hand.

And he would have no hesitation in leaving anybody out of the team - that includes myself! - if he thought it would be for the general good. So everybody is on edge now; we all know that our places are on the line.

That's what we needed. We lost the League championship last season because we lacked consistency. We'd score seven goals away from home one week, then lose at Anfield. It might have been exciting but it wasn't the old, familiar Liverpool pattern.

Arsenal won the title, and deservedly so, because they showed the resilience to go through a whole League campaign with only one defeat. That's a fantastic achievement, and they deserve every credit.

But they had better be warned . . . we want that trophy back; and we have a manager who will sweat blood - his and ours - to make sure we regain it!

A final word on Kenny, who suffered a lot of criticism for the way he resigned at a crucial part of the season. You won't find any complaints from me. The fact is that it took guts and common sense to do what he did.

If he'd carried on, when he was so obviously under strain, he might have finished up with a heart attack. What would people have said then?

He will always be a good pal of mine, and I wouldn't hesitate to ring him up and ask for any advice when I needed it. And I'll always remember the fantastic job he did for Liverpool, both as a player and as manager.

Kenny was the finest player I ever had the privilege of playing alongside. He had amazing skill and vision, and was also utterly unselfish. He created more goals for me than anyone. That's reason enough for me to be grateful. . . Thanks, Pal.

IAN RUSH

HONOURS EVEN

The 1990 Charity Shield match was fought out by Liverpool, the League champions, and Manchester United, the FA Cup holders, and the battle ended honours even, with the final scoreline 1–1. Which meant that the respective captains, Ronnie Whelan and Steve Bruce (in the absence of Alan Hansen and Bryan Robson) collected the Shield together. So each club would hold the trophy for six months.

The man who led Liverpool out at Wembley has served the club for close on 40 years, first as a player, then on the backroom side . . . Ronnie Moran, who had served loyally the managerial regimes of Bill Shankly, Bob Paisley, Joe Fagan and Kenny Dalglish, was allowed the honour of walking out at the head of the team, alongside United manager, Alex Ferguson and his men. It was a tribute from the then manager Kenny Dalglish, to his right-hand man which was thoroughly deserved.

Above: United's Gary Pallister dances attendance on John Barnes during the closely fought Charity Shield game at Wembley.

Left: Ronnie Moran, leads out the side before the 1990 Charity Shield game. Little did he know what surprises the season ahead held for him!

Right: Steve Bruce and Liverpool skipper, Ronnie Whelan *(right)* had to settle for a share of the 1990 Charity Shield – but Ronnie knows that possession is 9 tenths of the law!

Barnes is spot on

As for the game, United took the lead in the first half with a goal from Clayton Blackmore, but conceded an equalizer shortly after the restart – from a controversial penalty, as Gary Pallister challenged John Barnes and the England striker went down in the area. He picked himself up, dusted himself down . . . and slotted the spot-kick past 'keeper Les Sealey.

While United players claimed that the Pallister tackle had been fair, and that he had played the ball, John Barnes reckoned referee George Courtney had been right to award the penalty. 'I've got no doubts; as far as I'm concerned, it was a fair penalty,' he said. So the goal stood, and the contestants had to settle for a draw.

REDS SET THE STANDARD

Liverpool began season 1990–91 as they had left off the previous term . . . by maintaining a winning streak. Their first League match of the new campaign saw the Anfield Reds going to Bramall Lane to take on promoted Sheffield United, and while the Blades were unlucky to lose 'keeper Simon Tracey, few disputed Liverpool's right to victory.

Right: The Barclays League Championship flag is paraded by the Liverpool apprentices at the start of the new season while *(below right)* skipper Alan Hansen accepts the League Fair Play trophy from Gordon Taylor.

Ian Rush wasted no time in getting on the scoresheet for the '90–'91 season with two goals in the first two League games.

...RESULTS...

FA Charity Shield, 18 August

Liverpool 1	Manchester United 1
John Barnes (penalty)	*Clayton Blackmore*

Football League, 25 August

Sheffield United 1	Liverpool 3
Brian Deane	*John Barnes*
	Ray Houghton
	Ian Rush

Football League, 28 August

Liverpool 2	Nottingham Forest 0
Ian Rush	
Peter Beardsley	

League Position

	P	W	D	L	F	A	Pts	Position
Liverpool	2	2	0	0	5	1	6	First

Ironically, it was United right-back John Pemberton – an FA Cup semi-final hero for Crystal Palace against Liverpool only a few months earlier – who had to don the goalkeeper's jersey, on his debut for the Blades, and he finished up picking the ball out of the net three times, as Liverpool scored their 3–1 victory.

Barnes sets his sights

John Barnes opened the scoring just inside the hour, and though Brian Deane equalized almost immediately, Ray Houghton and Ian Rush struck to make a Liverpool win certain. So Rush and Barnes justified their rating as being among the favourites to finish up leading marksmen in the First Division, come the end of the season.

Forest felled

Nottingham Forest were the first visitors to Anfield, the following Tuesday night, and Liverpool saw them off with two goals – one from Rush, the other from Peter Beardsley, who had

missed the game at Sheffield on kick-off day. So the end of August saw Liverpool with maximum points from their two matches, and sitting at the top of the First Division table, while Ian Rush had collected a goal in each game.

SIX OF THE BEST

Six matches in September brought Liverpool victory every time out . . . and, not surprisingly, Kenny Dalglish finished up being voted the Barclays League Manager of the Month, as Liverpool wrote their names in the record books yet again.

First, they demolished Aston Villa, who had claimed the runners-up spot in the League the previous May, Peter Beardsley and John Barnes scoring the goals that set up a 2–1 success. Liverpool displayed such commanding form that England star David Platt was moved to say that they could already claim the championship of the Football League, after that performance.

United caned

There was another 2–1 victory, this time at Wimbledon's Plough Lane ground, where another Barnes goal and one from Ronnie Whelan did the damage; then came the always-tricky test against Manchester United at Anfield. This time out, though, it was tears, not cheers, for United, as Liverpool slammed four goals past them, with John Barnes scoring for the third game in succession and Peter Beardsley upstaging him with a hat-trick, to register five goals in three outings.

There was more to come, as well, because the Barnes-Beardsley combination broke Everton hearts in the derby game at Goodison Park, where Peter struck twice and John was on target with a penalty as Liverpool won 3–2. Everton took credit, though, for their fighting display after having been three goals adrift.

Crewe Alexandra in the Rumbelows-League Cup-tie shook Liverpool by taking an early lead, but eventually went down 5–1, as Steve McMahon equalized, then goals from Ian Rush (2), Gary Gillespie and Ray Houghton saw the Anfield Reds cruising through.

Right: John Barnes raps in another League goal during the 4–0 demolition of Alex Ferguson's Reds.

Left: Peter Beardsley salutes the Kop after his goal against Villa. It was the first of the September flood.

Record breakers

The last League match of the month was at Sunderland, and there Liverpool scored the only goal of the game, as Ray Houghton struck shortly before half-time. Once again Liverpool were back on song, and their victory meant that they had clocked up eight successive wins since kick-off day, with seven in the League contributing towards a club record.

By that stage, the bookies were making Liverpool 9–2 ON for the League title as they looked ahead to October and the prospect of overtaking Spurs' all-time record start of 11 successive victories.

· · · · · · · · · · RESULTS · · · · · · · · · · ·

Football League, 1 September

Liverpool 2	**Aston Villa 1**
Peter Beardsley	*David Platt*
John Barnes	

Football League, 8 September

Wimbledon 1	**Liverpool 2**
Alan Cork	*John Barnes*
	Ronnie Whelan

Football League, 16 September

Liverpool 4	**Manchester United 0**
Peter Beardsley (3)	
John Barnes	

Football League, 22 September

Everton 2	**Liverpool 3**
Andy Hinchcliffe	*Peter Beardsley (2)*
Glenn Hysen (o.g.)	*John Barnes*

Football League, 29 September

Sunderland 0	**Liverpool 1**
	Ray Houghton

Rumbelows-League Cup, 25 September

Liverpool 5	**Crewe Alexandra 1**
Ian Rush (2)	*Andy Sussex*
Steve McMahon	
Gary Gillespie	
Ray Houghton	

League Position

	P	W	D	L	F	A	Pts	Position
Liverpool	7	7	0	0	17	5	21	First

THE REDS GO MARCHING ON

The First Division table at the end of October bore exactly the same look as it had done during the previous nine weeks . . . Liverpool, still unbeaten, remained ahead of the pack, with nine victories and one draw from their ten matches, 22 goals scored, just 6 conceded, and a tally of 28 points, which put them four clear of their closest challengers, Arsenal.

Only one team – Norwich City – had managed to stem the relentless Red tide, and at Carrow Road a 1–1 draw had dented Liverpool's hopes of equalling or even overtaking Tottenham Hotspur's record start of eleven straight wins.

October began with the Anfield Reds scoring a 2–0 home win over Derby County, with the goals coming from Ray Houghton and Peter Beardsley. Houghton's goal was his third in as many matches. Three nights later, Liverpool went to Gresty Road for their Rumbelows – League Cup return with Crewe Alexandra, and won 4–1, to cruise into the third round.

Lucky Thirteenth

In that tie Ian Rush struck the fifteenth hat-trick of his career (his thirteenth with Liverpool), and took his tally of goals for the club to 250, while in the following League game at Norwich, he celebrated his 500th appearance in a red shirt, even if he didn't get his name on the scoresheet. That distinction went to Gary Gillespie, who struck after only two minutes.

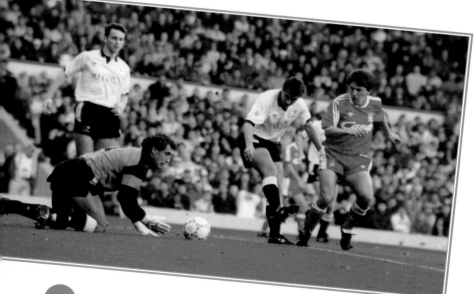

Above: Gary Gillespie, Liverpool's scorer, soars above the Norwich defence during the 1–1 away draw.

Above: Might is Wright! The England sweeper strides purposefully towards the ball during the October clash with Derby County at Anfield.

Below left: Peter Shilton gathers in safely, to deny a menacing Peter Beardsley.

Below: The midfield battle in full swing, as Steve McMahon slides in to win the ball for Liverpool.

...RESULTS...

Football League, 6 October

Liverpool 2	Derby County 0
Ray Houghton	
Peter Beardsley	

Football League, 20 October

Norwich City 1	Liverpool 1
Ruel Fox	Gary Gillespie

Football League, 27 October

Liverpool 2	Chelsea 0
Ian Rush	
Steve Nicol	

Rumbelows – League Cup, 9 October

Crewe Alexandra 1	Liverpool 4
Andy Sussex	Ian Rush (3)
	Steve Staunton

Rumbelows – League Cup, 31 October

Manchester United 3	Liverpool 1
Steve Bruce (pen)	Ray Houghton
Mark Hughes	
Lee Sharpe	

League Position

	P	W	D	L	F	A	Pts	Position
Liverpool	10	9	1	0	22	6	28	First

When Chelsea came to Anfield, John Barnes played a starring role until he had to retire through injury. He and Peter Beardsley joined forces, and Ian Rush finished off the move, to hit the target after only three minutes, and another bit of Barnes magic provided Steve Nicol with the chance to head goal no.2 with the game little more than a quarter of an hour old. That was the end of the scoring, though Chelsea had their moments, so Liverpool looked ahead to their next big test . . . the Rumbelows – League Cup – tie against Manchester United at Old Trafford on the last night of the month.

At the end of the night it was United who had cause to smile, for Liverpool – minus the injured John Barnes – failed to do themselves justice as they lost, 3–1. For Liverpool, it was the first reverse of the season – but they still led the way at the top of the First Division.

500 GAMES ✳ 250 GOALS

That's a *RUSH* Job!

Ian Rush had several things to celebrate, during season 1990-91, as he reached one footballing milestone after another . . . clocking up his 500th appearance; scoring his 200th goal in League football; and hitting the 300th goal of his career. Not to mention adding to his haul of hat-tricks.

Ian took his career total of games to 500 when he played for Liverpool against Norwich City at Carrow Road in October and, oddly enough, he scored the 200th League goal of his career when Norwich played at Anfield the following April.

In between, he took his overall tally of goals past the 250 mark in a Rumbelows-League Cup-tie against Crewe Alexandra – that was also the occasion for him to celebrate the 15th hat-trick of his glittering career – while the 300th goal came during the Anfield match against Crystal Palace in April, 1991.

The Rush haul of hat-tricks began when, as a schoolboy international, he scored three goals for Wales in a game against the Republic of Ireland lads. When he became a professional, he began to make a habit of hitting hat-tricks as he won his spurs with Liverpool.

In the League, for instance, he scored three goals against Notts County in season 1981–82, and the following term he did even better – four goals against Everton, hat-tricks against Coventry City and Notts County again. And in season 1983–84 he improved even upon that performance, because he hammered in five goals against Luton Town, four against Coventry and three against Aston Villa.

Season 1986–87 saw 'Rushy'

● *Left:* Ian Rush salutes the fans after a brace of goals against 'Spurs at White Hart Lane.

● *Right:* Ian Rush zeros in on the Real Sociedad goal during Kenny Dalglish's historic final appearance as a Liverpool player.

adding to his tally of League hat-tricks with three goals against Leicester City, while in the final of the Screen Sport Super Cup it was Everton who suffered from his marksmanship.

Ian Rush has made his mark, too, in the FA Cup, the European Cup and the Rumbelows-League Cup. Barnsley (season 1984–85) felt the impact of a hat-trick in the FA Cup sixth round at Oakwell, and Swansea City (season 1989–90) were the next FA Cup victims, while in the European Cup (season 1984–85) it was Benfica who wilted under the Rush onslaught. Then came that Rumbelows League Cup trio of goals against Crewe in season 1990–91.

No wonder, when you talk about Ian Rush and his habit of scoring goals, you tend to refer to these feats as being a 'Rush' job !

Right: The tormentor of Goodison. 'Rushy' goes up to celebrate yet another goal against the men in blue during the '89 derby win over Everton.

Below right: Ian Rush – superbly balanced and a picture of concentration.

Peter the
G·R·E·A·T !

Peter Beardsley may not have been singin' in the rain as he showed his paces during September, but he certainly made the opposition feel it was raining goals, as he struck seven in the course of four matches for Liverpool, and followed up in October with a stunning strike for England against Poland in the European-championship qualifier at Wembley.

Peter's first goal came in the 2–0 Anfield victory over Nottingham Forest, then he scored as Liverpool beat Aston Villa 2–1; and next he plundered a hat-trick against Manchester United, who went down to their heaviest defeat against their old adversaries in 65 years . . . before the days when Matt Busby wore a Liverpool jersey. And Sir Matt was there to see his old club triumph 4–0.

As Peter Beardsley rattled in those three goals against United, he also took his tally for Liverpool past the half-century mark, and he followed up by

sticking two more goals away in the Goodison Park derby game against Everton (which Liverpool won, 3–2). By the end of September Peter was staking his claim to an England recall, and he did get into the Wembley action as a substitute against Poland, hitting the superb late goal which brought a 2–0 victory.

All in all, Peter's dazzling performances during those weeks provided him with some very real compensation for the earlier days when he had found himself on the outside looking in, so far as the match action was concerned.

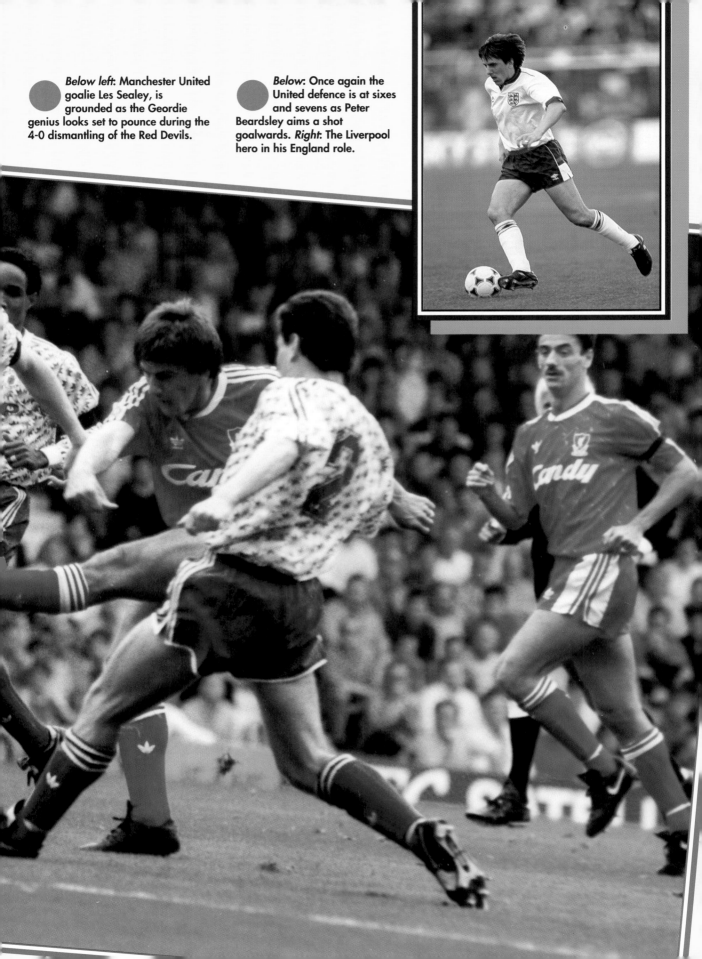

● *Below left*: Manchester United goalie Les Sealey, is grounded as the Geordie genius looks set to pounce during the 4-0 dismantling of the Red Devils.

● *Below*: Once again the United defence is at sixes and sevens as Peter Beardsley aims a shot goalwards. *Right*: The Liverpool hero in his England role.

ROCK-SOLID

Liverpool won three and drew one of their four Barclays League games in November – so, not surprisingly, they stayed ahead of the pack in the League championship stakes. Their first assignment was a tough test indeed . . . against Spurs (also undefeated) at White Hart Lane. In the event, David Burrows claimed the man-of-the-match award after a superb marking job on Paul Gascoigne, while Ian Rush collected a couple of goals and Peter Beardsley one, making the final scoreline 3–1 in favour of Liverpool.

Brucie takes a bow

After Tottenham, it was a case of 'bring on Luton Town' at Anfield. Liverpool struck four past them without reply, and after the game Bruce Grobbelaar stepped up to receive a cut-glass decanter – a presentation to mark his 500th appearance as Liverpool's last line of defence.

Above and left: The right man in the right place – 'Rushy' ghosts in behind the defence to poach one of his two goals against Luton Town.

...RESULTS...

Football League, 4 November

Tottenham Hotspur 1	Liverpool 3
Gary Lineker	*Ian Rush (2)*
	Peter Beardsley

Football League, 10 November

Liverpool 4	Luton Town 0
Ian Rush (2)	
Jan Molby (pen)	
Peter Beardsley	

Football League, 17 November

Coventry 0	Liverpool 1
	Peter Beardsley

Football League, 24 November

Liverpool 2	Manchester City 2
Ian Rush	*Mark Ward*
Ronny Rosenthal	*Niall Quinn*

League Position

	P	W	D	L	F	A	Pts	Position
Liverpool	14	12	2	0	32	9	38	First

Winners are red, losers are blue

One week later Liverpool ran out 1–0 winners at Coventry, where Peter Beardsley scored for the third game in succession. There was now just one more game to go in November, and Liverpool played host to Manchester City at Anfield. With the game just over an hour old, Mark Ward dispatched a penalty and Liverpool's first League defeat in 14 outings was on the cards. But

with only eight minutes remaining, Ian Rush scored, and four minutes later Ronny Rosenthal also turned up trumps.

However, City, though down, were not out; and with 60 seconds left on the clock striker Niall Quinn put the ball in the Liverpool net, to earn his side a point.

So the First Division table at the end of the month showed Liverpool at the top, with 38 points from 14 matches, and Arsenal still half a dozen points behind, while Spurs trailed by nine points. It certainly made the next big-game fixture an intriguing one !

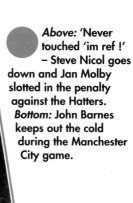

Above: 'Never touched 'im ref !' – Steve Nicol goes down and Jan Molby slotted in the penalty against the Hatters. *Bottom:* John Barnes keeps out the cold during the Manchester City game.

Tʜᴇ Pᴀᴄᴋ Cʟᴏsᴇs Iɴ

Liverpool began and ended the last month of 1990 with First Division matches in London, and – since both games were televised live – they had an audience of millions each time. On the first occasion the men from Anfield really suffered as Arsenal, fresh from a Rumbelows League Cup roasting by Manchester United (who had stuck six goals past them), came back with a fighting display which brought them a 3–0 victory over the champions.

Struggles at home

Liverpool then had two home matches in which to shrug off their disappointment, and they managed to make full use of their opportunities . . . though not without a battle. Bottom-of-the-table Sheffield United arrived at Anfield without a win but kept their opponents at bay for more than an hour before John Barnes and Ian Rush delivered the killer blows, much to the relief of the home fans. Then, when Southampton arrived at Anfield, a shock result was on the cards as Rod Wallace struck inside 20 minutes, to give the Saints the lead.

It was Ronny Rosenthal, making his first start to a League game, who levelled the score and then, almost on the stroke of half-time, put the Anfield Reds ahead . . . only for Wallace to crack home his second goal, shortly after the restart. Finally,

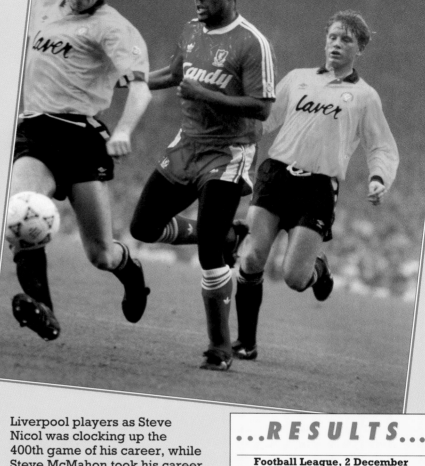

Left: Gary Gillespie. The Liverpool centre-back made his 200th appearance for the club in the Boxing Day game at Loftus Road.

Below left: Ronny Rosenthal heads for goal during the Southampton game. Having had to wait until 22 December to make his debut for the season, Ronny made up for lost time by netting twice.

Right: John Barnes tests the Blades' sharpness during the Reds' 2–0 home win.

Liverpool got the three points they were seeking as Ray Houghton rammed home a spectacular first-time shot, late in the game.

Then it was back to London for Liverpool, as they took on struggling Queen's Park Rangers in their next match at Loftus Road. John Barnes put them ahead, and it looked as if Liverpool (with Gary Gillespie making his 200th appearance for them) would have something to shout about . . . until Rangers got their name on the score sheet, with a controversial goal that brought them a much-needed point.

Palace pinch it

Liverpool then prepared to face up to high-riding Crystal Palace at Selhurst Park on the last Sunday of the month. In this game there were milestones for two more

Liverpool players as Steve Nicol was clocking up the 400th game of his career, while Steve McMahon took his career total to 450. However, it was not the happiest of days for Liverpool, because Palace struck through Mark Bright, just before the interval, and though Liverpool tried all they knew after the re-start, with Ronny Rosenthal adding his weight to the attack, they couldn't make the breakthrough.

So, as Arsenal had won 24 hours previously, it meant that the Anfield Reds led the Gunners by just one point (though still with a match in hand), while Palace had narrowed the gap between themselves and the champions to three points. Which made the championship chase look interesting indeed, as the First Division rivals looked to the matches on New Year's Day . . .

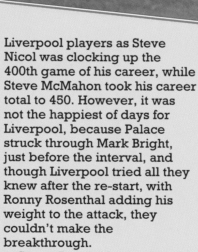

● *Above:* Bandits twelve o'clock high ? It looks like a natural for spot-the-ball, as David Speedie and two Evertonians engage in aerial combat at Anfield in February.

● *Left:* On a wing and a prayer. Battling Peter Beardsley heads towards another interception.

● *Right:* Now you see it, now you don't! Villa's Paul McGrath and Chris Price bewitched by the John Barnes magic.

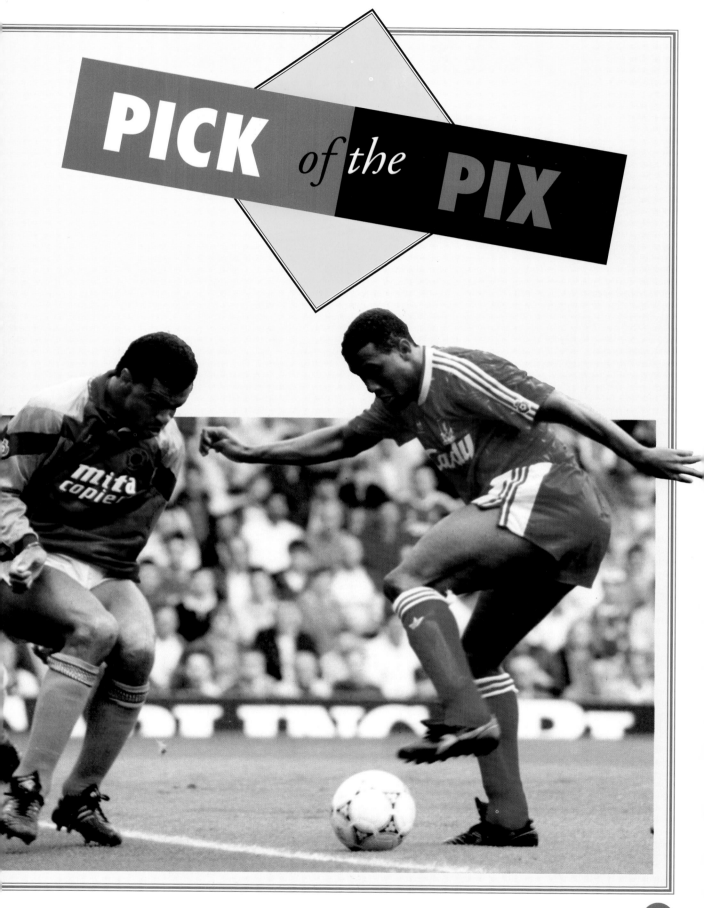

PICK of the PIX

RAY HOUGHTON

Most of Liverpool's players wear the same number week in, week out during the season – Glenn Hysen at No. 2, Steve Nicol at No. 4, Ronnie Whelan in the 'lucky' No. 5 strip he inherited from Ray Kennedy, Peter Beardsley at No. 7, Ian Rush at No. 9, John Barnes at No. 10, and Steve McMahon at No. 11.

Ray Houghton? – Yes, he usually does wear the No. 8 jersey – but in his time at Liverpool he's also switched from No. 7 to No. 8 to No. 9 to No. 10 to No. 11 to No. 12 and on to No. 14.

He made his first-team debut for Liverpool in the No. 9 shirt when he lined up for the game against Luton Town at Kenilworth Road on October 24, 1987; and when he scored his first goal for Liverpool at Wimbledon, early the following month, the number on his back was 12. By that time, he had also figured on the bench while wearing the No. 14 jersey, and later he had a run of 22 consecutive matches with No. 9 on his back.

The following season he kicked off at No. 9, switched to No. 8, then to No. 7, then to No. 10, changed again, to No. 8, and then to No. 9, went back to No. 10 . . . all in the course of the first eight matches. Later he wore the No. 11 shirt, alternated between Nos. 8, 9 and 10, was on the bench again wearing No. 14, switched back to No. 7, played 18 games wearing No. 9, then rounded off the season with two outings in the No. 7 shirt.

Right: Ray Houghton looks to be anticipating a painful challenge during the 1990 Charity Shield game at Wembley.

plays the NUMBERS GAME

● *Below left:* Ray Houghton shields the ball and looks to lay off as the Saints defence crowds in. Tight though the marking was, the elusive Liverpool man still found a way through to score during the game.

● *Below right:* Like a sprinter out of his blocks, Ray Houghton takes off down the left on another foray into enemy territory. His ability to take the ball forward at speed poses a constant threat to opposition defences.

In season 1990-91 things changed, as Ray pulled on the No. 8 jersey for the opening game, and stuck with that shirt while Liverpool were clocking up their record-beating, undefeated run. At last, it seemed, Ray Houghton had been able to stop playing the numbers game . . . but even if he did switch now and again, one thing remained constant . . . and that was no matter what number he wore his role was always to ply up and down the right-hand side of the field. Except of course, when he was cutting inside to make – or take – a scoring chance!

KENNY HANGS UP HIS BOOTS

When Kenny Dalglish took his testimonial match at Anfield more than 30,000 fans turned up to salute the man who, arguably, had been the most popular player in the long history of Liverpool Football Club. At the age of 39, Kenny – who had made his final First Division appearance in the game against Derby County the previous May – made his exit official early in the 1990–91 season as he peeled off the famous no.7 shirt at the end of the testimonial game and ran over to the section where the handicapped supporters were sitting. There he handed the jersey over to 76-year old Mrs Eileen Leffler, a lifelong Liverpool fan. Later she said proudly: 'Now I sleep with Kenny's shirt under my pillow!'

Left: Lifelong Liverpool fan Eileen Leffler. She was the lucky recipient of Kenny Dalglish's No.7 shirt at the end of his testimonial game versus Real Sociedad.

Real Sociedad, the crack Spanish club, provided the opposition for Liverpool, and this meant that John Aldridge, signed by Real the previous season, made a sentimental return to Anfield. But undoubtedly it was Kenny's night, as he laid on goals for Ian Rush and Steve McMahon, with Liverpool ending 3–1 winners. When Kenny took his leave, 15 minutes from the end, it marked 13 years of service as player and manager at Liverpool. No one realized it at the time, but it was also only a few months before his shock resignation as team manager brought his active association with the club to a close.

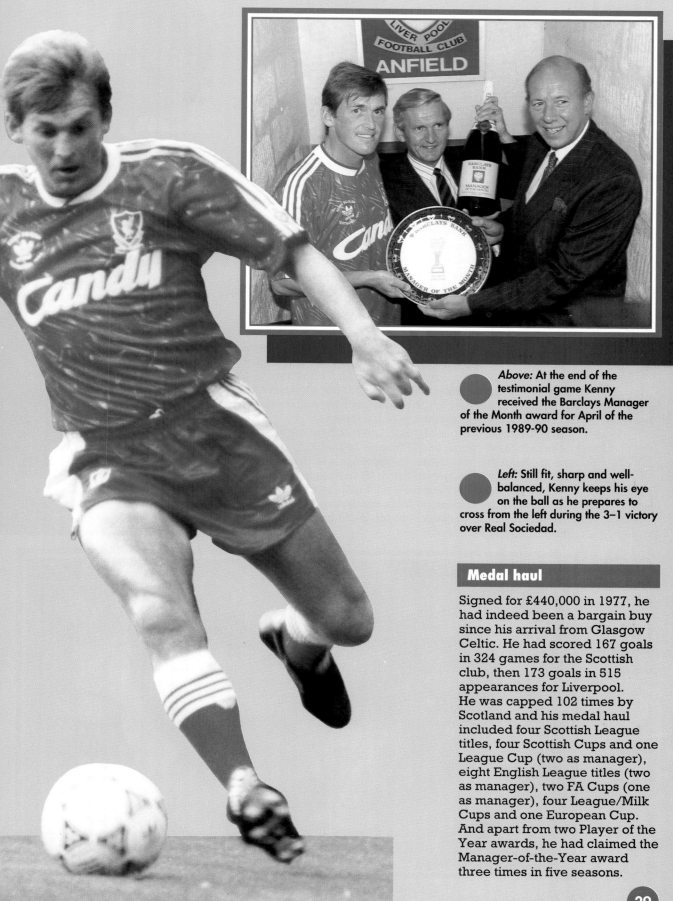

Above: At the end of the testimonial game Kenny received the Barclays Manager of the Month award for April of the previous 1989-90 season.

Left: Still fit, sharp and well-balanced, Kenny keeps his eye on the ball as he prepares to cross from the left during the 3–1 victory over Real Sociedad.

Medal haul

Signed for £440,000 in 1977, he had indeed been a bargain buy since his arrival from Glasgow Celtic. He had scored 167 goals in 324 games for the Scottish club, then 173 goals in 515 appearances for Liverpool. He was capped 102 times by Scotland and his medal haul included four Scottish League titles, four Scottish Cups and one League Cup (two as manager), eight English League titles (two as manager), two FA Cups (one as manager), four League/Milk Cups and one European Cup. And apart from two Player of the Year awards, he had claimed the Manager-of-the-Year award three times in five seasons.

BRUCIE'S CLEAN SHEETS

– just another day at the laundry!

Season by season, Bruce Grobbelaar goes out to play for Liverpool with the aim of finishing up as the 'keeper who has conceded fewest goals in the First Division – and his record of clean sheets throughout his career certainly stamps him as one of the most successful in English football.

Last season was his 10th at Liverpool, and the colourful Zimbabwe international could claim by the end of the campaign that he had kept a clean sheet – in other words – prevented the opposition from scoring no fewer than 17 times !

Considering that since he made his debut at the start of season 1981–82, when he was pitched into the action after the departure of Ray Clemence for Tottenham Hotspur, he has totalled more than 500 appearances for Liverpool, his record emphasises just how consistent he has been in staying at the top of the tree.

In seven seasons out of 10, Bruce has been an ever-present for Liverpool, and although Mike Hooper has had spells in the first team – a dozen games in season 1986–87, four the following term, 25 in season 1988–89 and 7 in 1990–91 – Liverpool's no.1 has defied his critics and resisted the challenge from inside the club to maintain his right to claim that his is the first name to go down on the team sheet.

Left: You could never call him a wallflower! Liverpool's Zimbabwe international makes his point forcefully whilst marshalling his defence.

Below left: As Liverpool's goalie, Bruce has handled more silverware over the years than the Royal Mint!

Right: Save! Bruce spreads out and covers his goal as an anxious David Burrows looks on.

Below right: Zimbabwe isn't exactly Down Under – but this is Bruce getting the feel of the turf as he celebrates another Wembley occasion.

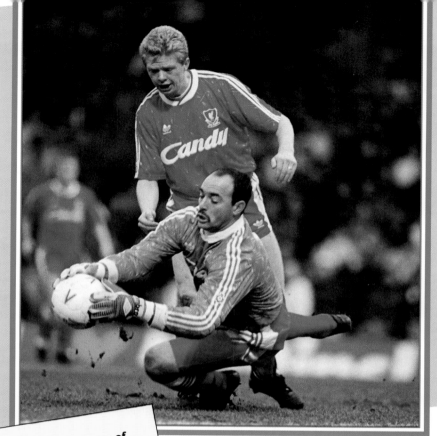

This is how the Grobbelaar story stacks up, in terms of games and clean sheets for Liverpool:

■ *Season 1981–82*: Ever-present (60 games) – 30 clean sheets (twice including run of five in successive matches).

■ *Season 1982–83*: Ever-present (59 games) – 26 clean sheets (twice including run of four in successive matches).

■ *Season 1983–84*: Ever-present (66 games) – 34 clean sheets (including a run of six in successive matches).

■ *Season 1984–85*: Ever-present (63 games) – 29 clean sheets (including three runs of three in successive matches).

■ *Season 1985–86*: Ever-present (63 games) – 24 clean sheets (including a run of six in successive matches).

■ *Season 1986–87*: 45 games – 21 clean sheets (including a run of six in successive matches).

■ *Season 1987–88*: 46 games – 23 clean sheets (including a run of six in successive matches).

■ *Season 1988–89*: 28 games – 14 clean sheets (including the abandoned FA Cup semi-final at Hillsborough and a run of four clean sheets in successive matches).

■ *Season 1989–90*: Ever-present (49 games) – 18 clean sheets (including a run of four in successive matches)

■ *Season 1990–91*: 42 games – 16 clean sheets (including the Charity Shield).

STRUGGLE FOR SUPREMACY

The first match in January, against Leeds at Anfield, began brightly for the opposition, so much so that they looked good enough to win the match; but gradually Liverpool got the upper hand, and goals from Ian Rush, John Barnes and Ronny Rosenthal killed off the challenge.

Below: The powerful Ronny Rosenthal shoots on the volley as the Anfield Reds gradually squeeze the life out of a lively Leeds outfit.

The third-round FA Cup-tie against Blackburn at Ewood Park then produced a shock, as Simon Garner gave Rovers the lead one minute into the second half, and the game was into its dying seconds when Blackburn's Mark Atkins, attempting to clear, managed only to put the ball past his own 'keeper.

Rovers Return

Blackburn threatened to give Liverpool a scare in the Anfield replay, too, but Ray Houghton, Ian Rush and Steve Staunton struck to make the final scoreline 3-0. Then in the League, Liverpool held Aston Villa to a scoreless draw in the Midlands, but lost a John Barnes-inspired lead against Wimbledon at Anfield, as Warren Barton rifled a 25-yard free-kick past Bruce Grobbelaar for the equaliser.

And so Liverpool took on Brighton in the fourth

round of the FA Cup – knowing that the Seagulls had been their jinx team in the competition before. However, when 'Rushy' struck twice in as many minutes, early in the second half, it seemed to be all up with Brighton . . . then it was Liverpool's turn to wilt as Mike Small (penalty) and John Byrne delivered telling strikes.

Brighton Rock

For the replay McMahon was back, while Ronnie Whelan returned after a lengthy spell out of action. It was McMahon who struck early to give Liverpool the edge, though Brighton rapped back with an equalizer. It was a game which went into extra time, one which became another cliffhanger, as Brighton snatched the lead, Liverpool restored the balance (through Ian Rush), then Steve McMahon emerged as the match-winner.

It wasn't plain sailing in the League, either, because Liverpool had lost the leadership of the First Division for the first time since the opening day of the season. For while the Reds were failing to subdue Wimbledon, the Gunners had put an end to Everton's unbeaten run by scoring the only goal of their encounter.

Above: Jimmy Carter, newly signed from Millwall, demonstrates his pace as he tests out the Dons' defence during the 1–1 draw at Anfield.

Below: Two-goal hero Ian Rush slots one in against a determined Brighton.

...R E S U L T S...

Football League, 1 January

Liverpool 3	Leeds United 0
John Barnes	
Ian Rush	
Ronny Rosenthal	

Football League, 12 January

Aston Villa 0	Liverpool 0

Football League, 19 January

Liverpool 1	Wimbledon 1
John Barnes	Warren Barton

FA Cup (Third Round), 5 January

Blackburn Rovers 1	Liverpool 1
Simon Garner	Mark Atkins (OG)

FA Cup (Third Round replay), 8 January

Liverpool 3	Blackburn Rovers 0
Ian Rush	
Ray Houghton	
Steve Staunton	

FA Cup (Fourth Round), 26 January

Liverpool 2	Brighton & HA 2
Ian Rush (2)	Mike Small
	John Byrne (pen)

FA Cup (Fourth Round Replay), 30 January

Brighton & HA 2	Liverpool 3
Mike Small	Steve McMahon (2)
John Byrne	Ian Rush

League Position

	P	W	D	L	F	A	Pts	Position
Liverpool	22	15	5	2	42	17	50	Second

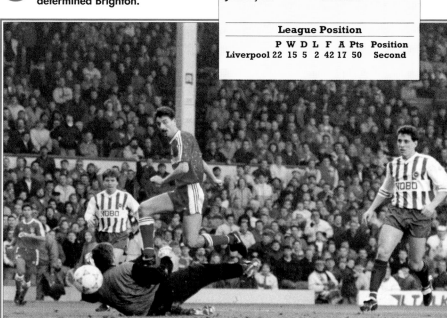

DEMOLITION

Season 1990-91 saw Liverpool and Everton meeting no fewer than FIVE times . . . twice in the First Division derby games, and three times in the FA Cup. Everton finally came out on top in the Cup but, in the League clashes, it was an entirely different story .

The first derby game took place at Goodison in September and ended with the Anfield Reds scoring a 3-2 victory. Of the three Liverpool goals, two came from a sparkling Peter Beardsley, and the other from a man who's also been a regular marksman for the Reds - John Barnes. He beat Neville Southall from the penalty spot.

It was February when the second derby game came round, and for this game at Anfield the Toffees were under new management. The charismatic Howard Kendall had returned from Spain, with Colin Harvey reverting to his former role of No.2.

But, whatever the management re-shuffles, the result was the same - another victory for Liverpool. This time by a 3-1 margin. And, once again, the Anfield Reds had a two-goal hero . . . a player who was among the last batch of signings by Kenny Dalglish before he resigned as Liverpool's manager.

David Speedie, signed from Coventry City for a reported £675,000, followed up a point-saving performance against Manchester United at Old Trafford by striking twice against Everton . . . and midfielder Jan Molby was also on the mark. Indeed the big Dane's shot struck Speedie's heel on its way into the net and, technically, the Scottish international could have claimed a hat-trick. However, he didn't, and satisfied himself instead with striking twice in a three-minute spell after the restart, to bring the home fans to their feet and ensure that Liverpool finished up with six points from the two games against their neighbours and closest rivals, as they sought to prevent Arsenal from taking back their League-championship crown.

DERBY

Two-goal hero David Speedie heads narrowly wide, and Neville Southall hits the Anfield mud during the second leg of the derby game.

A ROLLER-COASTER MONTH

All inside the shortest month of the year, Liverpool experienced just about everything the football fates could throw at them – certainly the club and the fans shared contrasting emotions, as together, they rode a switchback of highs and lows.

On the first Saturday in February, Liverpool were second to Arsenal; on the second Saturday, they leap-frogged to the top; but on the last Saturday they had surrendered the lead to the Gunners once again.

Below: David Speedie and Steve Bruce tear up the Old Trafford turf during the hotly contested 1–1 draw. Speedie scored in this game and against Everton (*right*) where Hysen hails the goal as Southall stands in disbelief.

A Speedie repayment

On the transfer front, having signed Jimmy Carter and Jamie
Redknapp, Liverpool completed a treble with the arrival of £650,000
David Speedie from Coventry City, and the Scottish international
swiftly repaid a chunk of his fee by scoring a point-saving goal, as
he made his debut against Manchester United at Old Trafford – then
he went one better when Everton tried their luck in the return derby
game at Anfield. Speedie struck twice, with Jan Molby also a
marksman as Liverpool chalked up a 3–1 victory to make it a double
over their old rivals from across the park.

Eight days later Liverpool and Everton met again, this time in the
fifth round of the FA Cup, and after a scoreless stalemate at Anfield
the teams shared eight goals at Goodison, where the tie went to
extra time. Four times Liverpool swept into the lead, with goals from
the recalled Peter Beardsley (2), Ian Rush and John Barnes, yet still
they failed to clinch victory, so the 38,000 crowd went home
wondering what would happen in a second replay – a replay which,
once again, took place at Goodison, since Everton had won the toss
for home advantage.

However, in between the first and second replays there was even
more drama, as the news broke from Anfield that manager Kenny
Dalglish had resigned. The morning after that 4–4 FA Cup cliff –
hanger, Dalglish told the board the time had come for him to quit.

KENNY

...RESULTS...

Football League, 3 February

Manchester United 1	Liverpool 1
Steve Bruce (pen)	*David Speedie*

Football League, 9 February

Liverpool 3	Everton 1
David Speedie (2)	*Pat Nevin*
Jan Molby	

Football League, 23 February

Luton Town 3	Liverpool 1
Iain Dowie (2)	*Jan Molby (pen)*
Kingsley Black	

FA Cup – Fifth round, 17 February

Liverpool 0	Everton 0

FA Cup – Fifth round replay, 20 February

Everton 4	Liverpool 4
Graeme Sharp (2)	*Peter Beardsley (2)*
Tony Cottee (2)	*Ian Rush*
	John Barnes

FA Cup – Fifth round second replay, 27 February

Everton 1	Liverpool 0
Dave Watson	

League Position

	P	W	D	L	F	A	Pts	Position
Liverpool	25	16	6	3	47	22	54	Second

BOWS OUT

FEBRUARY 21 was a fateful day for Liverpool during season 1990–91, as Kenny Dalglish broke the bombshell news that, with three years of his contract still to run, he wanted to quit as manager. Despite attempts to persuade him to change his mind, Liverpool's board had to accept the decision and bow to the inevitable. So on the morning of Friday, February 22, they called a Press conference and informed a stunned football world of what had happened.

Chairman Noel White stressed that the parting of the ways was amicable – 'I'm still a Kenny Dalglish fan,' he declared – and Dalglish himself maintained that his decision to quit had come about because of the pressures involved in the constant search for success. Like the Liverpool chairman, he said the parting was amicable, and told his audience that up to that point everything he had done had been with with the interests of the club foremost in his mind . . . now, for once, this was a decision for Kenny Dalglish.

As the chairman made it clear that Kenny would always be welcome back, at any time, the realization grew that Liverpool and, arguably, their most successful manager, had indeed come to a parting of the ways; and as Dalglish drove out through the famous Shankly gates he was said to have been close to tears.

Ronnie takes over

But life and football must go on, and Liverpool announced that Ronnie Moran, the first-team coach and an Anfield man for more than 40 years, would take over as acting manager. His first job was to pick the team for the League game at Luton, and after

Liverpool had lost, 3–1, he faced the media men and managed to smile, despite the disappointment of the day. No recriminations, no inquest on the spot – that was his verdict. The talking would be done on the Monday morning, then the players would get down to preparing for the second FA Cup replay against Everton at Goodison Park.

That game ended with Liverpool suffering yet another setback, because although they played well – 'keeper Neville

Left: An anxious looking Kenny Dalglish peers from the Liverpool dug-out and (above) is pictured with Liverpool chairman Noel White on the day the resignation bombshell broke.

Southall came to Everton's rescue several times – they lost by the only goal of the match . . . and, ironically, it was scored by a one-time Liverpool reserve – team player, Dave Watson. So that left the Anfield Reds with just the League title as their remaining target.

39

Liverpool's FA Cup trail in season 1990–91 began at Blackburn Rovers' Ewood Park on Saturday, January 5, and ended six matches later, in the fifth round, just a few hundred yards from their own Anfield home . . . across the park at Goodison. All of which meant that they failed to get to Wembley – yet they had played one more game than it would have taken for them to win the FA Cup in what might be called 'straight sets'.

Both the third and fourth round games against Blackburn and then Brighton went to hard-fought replays, and when Liverpool eventually won through they found themselves facing a meeting with their greatest rivals, Everton. In fact, the teams were scheduled to meet twice at Anfield in the space of nine days, because before the Cup-tie came a League fixture.

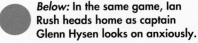

Merseyside Classic

Everton lost that one 3–1, but they played well enough in the Cup-tie to take Liverpool back to Goodison for a replay. If there had been no goals in the first Cup duel, the second provided a veritable feast and, arguably, the finest Merseyside Cup occasion of all time. Four times Liverpool led the Blues, and four times Everton responded with goals, to salvage a second replay.

Peter Beardsley struck twice for Liverpool, Ian Rush was on the mark – as usual! – and John Barnes got his name on the scoresheet as well. Each time as the ball went past Everton 'keeper Neville

Above: Everton 'keeper Neville Southall is a helpless spectator as John Barnes finds the net in the first replay game.

Below: In the same game, Ian Rush heads home as captain Glenn Hysen looks on anxiously.

Their Cup Runneth Over!

Southall, it seemed that this one would be the winner. But Graeme Sharp (2) and substitute Tony Cottee (2) ensured that Everton lived to fight another night.

Everton winning the toss for choice of venue, the second replay also took place at Goodison on February 27, and an eager audience waited to see what would unfold. By that time, Kenny Dalglish was no longer Liverpool manager, and Ronnie Moran had stepped up from coach to become caretaker team boss.

Liverpool played well enough, but they just couldn't stick the chances away; and the irony of it was that when a goal did come it was scored for Everton by a former Liverpool reserve-team player, Dave Watson.

So Liverpool's bid to take both the League title and the FA Cup had been scuttled and Everton, at last, had triumphed after having been vanquished by their old foes in two FA Cup finals during the 1980s. Now, for Liverpool, it was a case of concentrating all their efforts on the championship as they faced the fact that, for them, the Cup was over.

Left: It takes two to tango! Peter Beardsley joins Ian Rush in celebrating Liverpool's third goal in the sensational 4–4 draw at Goodison.

Thanks for THE MEMORIES

Hard on the heels of the shock news that manager Kenny Dalglish had resigned came the announcement that team-captain Alan Hansen was hanging up his boots, after a lengthy battle to overcome injury problems. So ended a career which, through 14 years, had been crowned with success and, indeed, some record-breaking feats.

It was Alan Hansen who led Liverpool to their classic League -title/FA Cup double in season 1985–86, only two seasons after he had gone through a 66-match campaign as an ever-present and collected a unique set of medals then . . . the League championship, the European Cup and the League – Milk Cup.

Signed from Partick Thistle in 1977, Alan admitted that when he first arrived at Anfield 'the summit of my ambition was just to play in the first team.' He swiftly achieved this and, as he said, 'once you get into the team, it becomes a roller-coaster . . . 'so much so that as he helped the club scale new peaks of achievement, he could claim a medal haul which compared with the best.

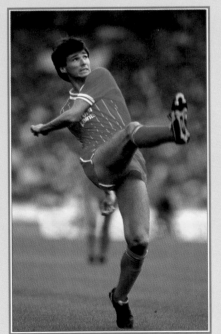

Right: Alan Hansen salutes the Kop on the day he clinched his eighth League championship medal - the last in a glorious Anfield career that spanned 14 years.

Left: A cool defender who also possessed silky skills, Hansen clears the lines during a Manchester United attack in 1983.

In his first season he totalled 27 first-team games, including the 1978 European Cup final against FC Bruges at Wembley. Like Phil Neal, Alan Hansen picked up three winner's medals in the European Cup, eight in the League championship, two in the FA Cup and four in successive seasons in the League – Milk Cup competition.

In season 1978–79 he figured in the Liverpool side which conceded a record low number of League goals (16) as they claimed the title, and he set a record for derby-game appearances against Everton when at Goodison Park in September, 1989, he overtook Ian Callaghan's 31 – game total. At the start of the 1990s he had become the club's longest–serving player, and when he bowed out he had totalled 620 appearances for the club and 728 overall in top-class football.

For their £100,000 expenditure, Liverpool got themselves a bargain buy, and the fans were quick to appreciate the cultured brand of football which 'Jocky' Hansen displayed so consistently . . . in fact, he almost made an art form of defending. And from his host of admirers, this was the final verdict: 'Alan Hansen, thanks for the memories . . .'

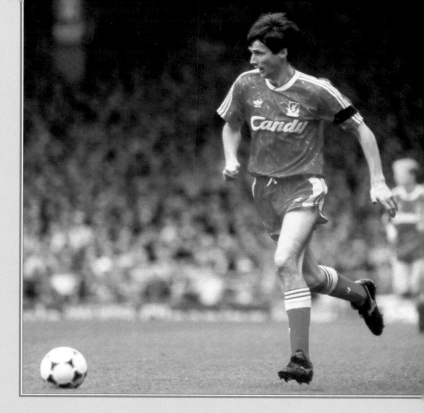

Above: Always comfortable in possession, Alan Hansen exhibits that characteristic, long-legged stride as he brings the ball forward against Nottingham Forest.

Below: (l to r) Rosenthal, Rush, Whelan, Hansen and Barnes pictured with the 1989/90 League championship trophy.

OUT OF THE FRYING PAN

He's no stranger to the dug out, but, for the first time, Ronnie Moran experiences the responsibility of management in the aftermath of the Dalglish resignation.

Inset: Jan Molby helps to lift the gloom as he sets Liverpool on the road to their first victory of the post-Dalglish era, against Manchester City at Maine Road.

One thing is for sure . . . Ronnie Moran doesn't like losing. His first appearance for Liverpool as a player was in a League match against Derby County at the Baseball Ground on November 22, 1952. Liverpool lost by the odd goal in five, and when reminded of this fact nearly 40 years later, Ronnie's answer was short and direct: 'Oh, I don't remember things like that!'

After the shock resignation of Kenny Dalglish as manager, Ronnie had been in charge for three games before he finally saw his team win. They had lost in the League at Luton in the first game, then again against Everton in the second FA Cup replay at Goodison; and had played well, but lost again, when they met Arsenal in the League return at Anfield.

The talk had been that the club were on the verge of bringing back former Anfield favourite John Toshack from Real Sociedad, and all the time Ronnie Moran - named as no more than caretaker manager, was trying to get to grips with the problems besetting the Anfield club. Not least, the injury situation which had robbed Liverpool of key midfield men Steve McMahon and Ronnie Whelan.

In the event, three things happened, within a short space of time : Liverpool enjoyed some good fortune as they won 3-0 at Maine Road; Toshack decided in favour of honouring his commitment to his Spanish club; and Ronnie Moran remained in charge of team affairs at Liverpool until the arrival of Graeme Souness.

Bill Shankly, Bob Paisley, Joe Fagan, Kenny Dalglish . . . Ronnie had seen them all come and go, as managers; and he had served loyally under all of them, as well. And as events unfolded, Ronnie gave the new manager and Liverpool Football Club a pledge of continued loyalty. As he said before the news of the new appointment broke: 'Given the opportunity, I'd still want to stay at Anfield. I don't want to leave . . . I've been here all my working life.' So once again, he resumed his familiar role as he got down to work alongside manager No. 5.

QUIZ

Questions

1 Here's a shot from the Charity Shield game between Liverpool and Manchester United. Can you name the referee?

2 You'll recognize the Liverpool man . . . but can you name the goalkeeper?

3 These two men have played together for England . . . who are they?

4 Can you name the man who's giving Peter Beardsley treatment here?

5 It's John Barnes in aerial action - but can you name the opposition?

6 Here's Ian Rush in a duel for possession. Which team provided the opposition?

7 Ronny Rosenthal scored seven goals in eight League games towards the end of season 1989-90 . . . but did he get a championship medal?

8 No cheating by looking back! Who scored for Liverpool in the 1990 Charity Shield game at Wembley?

9 Who scored Liverpool's first League goal of season 1990-91?

10 Now. . . which player scored Liverpool's first League goal of the season at Anfield?

11 Champions Liverpool beat runners-up Aston Villa 2-1 at Anfield, at the start of season 1990-91. Who scored for Liverpool?

12 And which player scored Aston Villa's goal?

13 How many times did Kenny Dalglish claim the Manager-of-the-Year award?

14 And how many times has John Barnes won the Footballer-of-the-Year award since his arrival at Anfield?

Quiz Answers

1 George Courtney
2 Nigel Spink (Aston Villa)
3 Peter Beardsley and Des Walker
4 Liverpool coach Roy Evans
5 Nottingham Forest
6 Aston Villa
7 No – he didn't qualify
8 John Barnes (Penalty)
9 John Barnes again
10 Ian Rush
11 Peter Beardsley and John Barnes
12 David Platt
13 Three times
14 Twice

Here's to the
NEXT HUNDRED!

Liverpool F.C. was formed in 1892 . . . which means that the club is about to celebrate 100 years of footballing history. It has been a century during which the club has become the most successful in British soccer and world famous to boot!

Here are just some of the records behind the success!

Appearances:

Ian Callaghan made his League debut as a 17-year-old, replacing his great idol Billy Liddell, and he went on to overtake Liddell's record of 532 appearances in competitive matches for the club. By the time he left Liverpool in 1978 he had clocked up over 850 appearances.

Ian Callaghan, one of a long line of great Liverpool wingers, flanked by Bill Shankly *(left)* and Bob Paisley *(right)*.

Championships and Cups:

Liverpool have won the Football League Championship 18 times - easily an all-time record; they have also won four FA Cups, four European Cups, four League-Milk Cups and two UEFA Cups. This collection of cups is unparalleled in English soccer.

Defensive Records:

In 1893-4 Liverpool won 22 and drew 6 of their 28 games, thus becoming only the second club to go through a season unbeaten (Preston are the others). In their championship-winning season of 1978-79 Liverpool conceded a record low 16 league goals.

Everton:

Liverpool and Everton have met almost 150 times in League matches, twice in the final of the FA Cup, once in the final of the Milk Cup, and once in the two-legged final of the Screen Sport Super Cup. Liverpool won all four of those finals. Three players have special reasons for remembering derby games. . . Alan Hansen, Ian Rush and Steve McMahon. Hansen holds the record for appearances against Everton in derby games; Rush holds the record for goals; and McMahon can proudly claim to be the only Scouser to have captained both Liverpool and Everton.

● *Above:* 'Crazy Horse', otherwise known as Emlyn Hughes, lifts the European Cup as Liverpool captain in May 1978.

● *Right:* Liverpool F.C. believe in keeping the carpenters busy. The ever-expanding trophy cabinet at Anfield.

Goals:

Roger Hunt holds the Liverpool scoring record, with 285 League and Cup goals in just under 500 appearances between 1959 and 1970. He scored 245 League goals in his Liverpool career and scored 41 in all competitions in season 1961-62. The previous record holder was Gordon Hodgson, who played from 1925-1936, during which he hit 233 League goals and eight in cup-ties. He has recently been overtaken by Ian Rush who has now scored 270 League and Cup goals for Liverpool.

Home Record:

In season 1893-94 Liverpool won all their 15 home League matches at Anfield. Later there were several occasions when the team went through a season without losing a home game, and, indeed, they earned a reputation for being virtually invincible at Anfield.

Internationals:

Many Liverpool footballers have played for their respective countries, and Emlyn Hughes became the club's most capped player with England - he won 59 caps while at Liverpool and three more during his days at Wolves. Kenny Dalglish was capped 102 times for Scotland during his career with Liverpool and Glasgow Celtic. Liverpool's current squad have a wide international pedigree, the club boasting players who have played for England, Scotland, Wales, Eire, Israel, Denmark, Sweden and Zimbabwe.

Managers:

Liverpool have had just 13 managers during the whole of their history. Here is the list - W.E. Barclay, Tom Watson, David Ashworth, Matt McQueen, George Patterson, George Kay, Don Welsh, Phil Taylor, Bill Shankly, Bob Paisley, Joe Fagan, Kenny Dalglish and Graeme Souness.

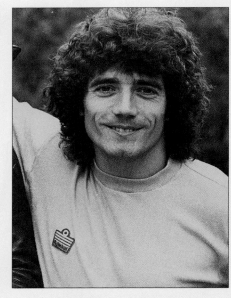

Above: Kevin Keegan, one of the all-time great Liverpool and England forwards.
Right: This is Anfield !

Great Scot ! Three Liverpool and Scotland internationals captured in one frame. *(l to r)* Graeme Souness, Alan Hansen and Kenny Dalglish with the 1982 League – Milk Cup trophy.

Famous Names:

No club in British football has had more famous names on its books, going back to Elisha Scott, one of the greatest goalkeepers of all time. Much more recently men like Tommy Lawrence, Ray Clemence and Bruce Grobbelaar have followed in Scott's footsteps. In defence there were Alex Raisbeck, 'Tiny' Bradshaw, Donald McKinley, Chris Lawler, Tommy Smith, Ron Yeats; in midfield men like Phil Taylor, Graeme Souness, Terry McDermott; on the wing Billy Lacey, 'Polly' Hopkin, Billy Liddell, Peter Thompson, Steve Heighway and Ian Callaghan; and strikers such as Harry 'Smiler' Chambers, Jack Parkinson, Alfred Stubbins, Kevin Keegan, Kenny Dalglish and Ian Rush.

Left: The European Champions Cup about to be paraded by Ray Clemence *(left)* and Emlyn Hughes *(right)* at the start of the '78 -'79 season. Terry McDermott brings up the rear.

51

MIXED FORTUNES

Five matches in March brought a mixed bag of results for Liverpool, as Arsenal knocked them off the top of the First Division table, saw their rivals leap-frog back into pole position, then reversed that process on the last Saturday of the month as the Gunners won at Derby while Liverpool were losing at Anfield.

Gunning for the Championship

Sunday, March 3, was the day that Arsenal tried their luck at Anfield. . . and found it was in, as Paul Merson scored the only goal to bring them three precious points. The following Saturday, though, Liverpool gave caretaker manager Ronnie Moran his first victory as they plundered three goals against Manchester City at Maine Road.

Back with a Vengeance

Bruce Grobbelaar missed the remaining three matches of the month because he had a broken finger, so Mike Hooper stood in, and Liverpool won two of those matches - a somewhat scrambled, 2-1 success against lowly Sunderland at Anfield, then a sparkling, 7-1 triumph over bottom-club Derby County at the Baseball Ground, where Ian Rush celebrated his 450th appearance in a red jersey with a goal, and John Barnes and Steve Nicol each scored twice.

That was Liverpool's biggest away victory in the League since 1896 - and, oddly enough,that was against a close neighbour of Derby's . . . Burton Swifts.

The last Saturday of the month saw Liverpool kicking off as the First Division top-dogs and ending the day playing second fiddle, because struggling Queen's Park Rangers - who had lost 13 and drawn just one of the 14 matches previously played at Anfield - provided the shock result of the day, as they won 3-1.

And, since Arsenal had won 2-0 against Derby County at the Baseball Ground, it left Liverpool with eight games to go and the knowledge that they had it all to do, if they were to retain the championship.

The only really good news in the month had been that forward ace John Barnes had unequivocally committed himself to a further year at Liverpool, temporarily turning his back on the temptation to pursue his profession in sunnier climes. This was the news the Anfield faithful had wanted to hear.

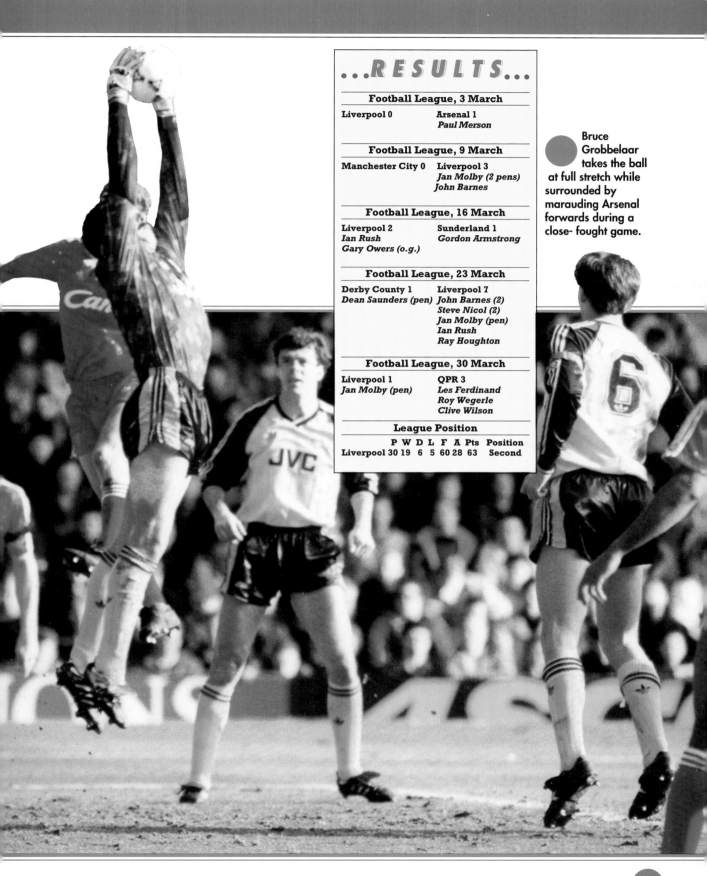

...R E S U L T S...

Football League, 3 March

Liverpool 0	Arsenal 1
	Paul Merson

Football League, 9 March

Manchester City 0	Liverpool 3
	Jan Molby (2 pens)
	John Barnes

Football League, 16 March

Liverpool 2	Sunderland 1
Ian Rush	*Gordon Armstrong*
Gary Owers (o.g.)	

Football League, 23 March

Derby County 1	Liverpool 7
Dean Saunders (pen)	*John Barnes (2)*
	Steve Nicol (2)
	Jan Molby (pen)
	Ian Rush
	Ray Houghton

Football League, 30 March

Liverpool 1	QPR 3
Jan Molby (pen)	*Les Ferdinand*
	Roy Wegerle
	Clive Wilson

League Position

	P	W	D	L	F	A	Pts	Position
Liverpool	30	19	6	5	60	28	63	Second

Bruce Grobbelaar takes the ball at full stretch while surrounded by marauding Arsenal forwards during a close-fought game.

A NEW START?

If February was sensational for the departure of Kenny Dalglish, April was equally dramatic because it saw the arrival of Graeme Souness as the new manager and the announcement that the Anfield Reds would be back on the European circuit the following season - just in time to celebrate the club's centenary.

Ronnie Moran's tenure as the man in charge of team affairs ended in a matter of a few hours on April 16th, as the news broke about the impending shock exit from Ibrox of Graeme Souness, after a successful spell as manager of Glasgow Rangers, because he drove straight from a Press conference in Glasgow to one in Liverpool - by eight o'clock that evening, he was at Anfield being instantly installed as the new manager.

The Brilliant and the Brittle

So Souness arrived just in time to take charge for the next two home games - against Norwich City and Crystal Palace - which were crucial if Liverpool were to make up ground on Arsenal in the chase for the championship. Liverpool, having lost 1-0 (and rather unluckily) at Southampton on the first day of the month, and having drawn (rather luckily) against Coventry City at Anfield, had shown the brittle side of their nature during their third League game in April, at Elland Road . . . after storming into a 4-0 lead, they allowed their opponents to claw their way back into the game and, in the end, Liverpool just hung on to win by the odd goal in nine.

At that stage Arsenal were looking clear favourites for the title, but 24 hours after Liverpool's success at Leeds, the Gunners were being knocked off the Wembley trail by their great north-London rivals ,

Tottenham Hotspur, who thus demolished Arsenal's dream of a League-title-FA-Cup double. And a few nights later, at Highbury, a 2-0 lead against Manchester City was whittled away as City finished up all square.

Below: Steve Staunton *(right)* looks concerned as Ian Rush tumbles over an outstretched 'Palace leg. Peter Beardsley *(left)* takes avoiding action.

The Pundits Ponder

So the arrival of Graeme Souness at Liverpool gave the Anfield club a boost and - once again - had the pundits speculating as to whether or not the title race was still on. To be sure, Liverpool still had to win all of their remaining matches . . . but if Arsenal should slip, they could let Liverpool back in.

The first two matches under the new managerial regime brought team changes - and two victories. Out went skipper Glenn Hysen, as Graeme Souness opted for a back-three line of Gary Gillespie, Jan Molby and Gary Ablett, with Steve Nicol (the new captain) playing wide on the right, and the midfield being completed by Ray Houghton, Steve Staunton and David Burrows, with a front three of Peter Beardsley, Ian Rush and John Barnes.

Norwich City went down 3-0 at Anfield, and Ian Rush duly clocked up the 200th League

Above: John Barnes looks about to lose possession during this tussle with the Norwich defence. Compensation came later with a goal in the 3-0 victory.

goal of his career; and when Crystal Palace suffered the same fate three nights later, 'Rushy' took his career total of goals to 300, while John Barnes hit his second goal in successive games. So Liverpool ended the month still on Arsenal's heels, though they remained three points adrift after the Gunners had beaten Queen's Park Rangers.

That left Arsenal and Liverpool with three matches each to play in May . . . Arsenal at Sunderland, and home to Manchester United and Coventry City; Liverpool at Chelsea and Nottingham Forest, with the final match at home against Tottenham Hotspur. The Gunners had a superior goal difference, too . . . so Liverpool knew they needed to win all three matches, while hoping for a slip by their rivals.

...RESULTS...

Football League, 1 April

Southampton 1	Liverpool 0
Matthew Le Tissier	

Football League, 9 April

Liverpool 1	Coventry City 1
Ian Rush	Micky Gynn

Football League, 13 April

Leeds United 4	Liverpool 5
Lee Chapman (3)	John Barnes (2)
Carl Schutt	Ray Houghton
	Jan Molby (pen)
	David Speedie

Football League, 20 April

Liverpool 3	Norwich 0
John Barnes	
Ray Houghton	
Ian Rush	

Football League, 23 April

Liverpool 3	Crystal Palace 0
Ian Rush	
John Barnes	
Eddie McGoldrick (og)	

League Position

	P	W	D	L	F	A	Pts	Position
Liverpool	35	22	7	6	72	34	73	Second

RETURN OF A LEGEND

The arrival of Graeme Souness as Liverpool's new manager sent shock waves around the world of football - because people in the game were swift to admit that (not for the first time) Liverpool had pulled off a major coup. They had done it when they signed Kenny Dalglish to replace Kevin Keegan . . . they had done it again when they re-signed Ian Rush from Juventus . . . and now they were replacing Dalglish as team boss by persuading one of their former greats - and one of Kenny Dalglish's closest friends in football - to take on the giant-sized task.

Souness departed from Glasgow Rangers amid a storm of controversy, because it had been assumed that he was there, if not for life, at least for the next few years. Indeed he had signed a five-year contract with Rangers in May, 1989, become director-manager in November of that year, and was believed to have a substantial shareholding in the Ibrox club. Furthermore, he had seemingly indicated, shortly after Dalglish had resigned, that his name could be erased from the list of candidates.

But - and not for the first time in his career - he made front-page and back-page headlines

A delighted Graeme Souness hoists the 1984 European Champions Cup during his playing days for Liverpool.

as he turned his back on arguably the top job in Scottish football to confront the challenge of arguably the top job south of the Border.

Edinburgh-born, Souness was just a month short of his 38th birthday when he made the sensational switch from the blue of Rangers back to the red of Liverpool, the club he had skippered and for which he had played with such distinction. His playing career had taken him first from Scotland to Tottenham Hotspur, when he was a youngster trying to make his way in the game, then North to Ayresome Park and Middlesborough, West to Liverpool and Anfield, further afield to Sampdoria in Italy, back to Britain and Glasgow Rangers . . . and now the wheel was turning full circle.

During his playing career Liverpool had paid Middlesborough a then club-record fee of £352,000 when

Souness was signed in January, 1978. And he said at the time: 'Any player would give his right arm to play for Liverpool.' Three years on and he was being handed the captaincy . . . 'the biggest honour I've had in my football career' was how he described it.

Hailed as Liverpool's midfield maestro, Souness orchestrated the moves with a silken touch tempered by a streak of steel, and in his six years with the club they won the League title five times (including a hat-trick from 1982 – 1984), the European Cup three times, and the League Milk Cup four times (in successive years). Apart from making goals such as the one he created for Kenny Dalglish – Liverpool's European Cup match-winner in 1978 – Souness scored some vital ones himself. The 1984 Milk-Cup replay winner against Everton, for instance, and one of the goals in the famous 1984 European Cup-final penalty

shoot-out against AS Roma.

By the time he was leaving Liverpool, he had totalled 352 appearances and scored 56 goals, and the Anfield club collected £650,000 from Sampdoria, with whom he stayed two years.

Rangers had appointed him as their player-manager in 1986, and he had led them to success three times in the championship - with a fourth title looming - and four times in the Skol League Cup. So in moving back to Anfield he was taking up a tremendous challenge, as Liverpool sought to come from behind in the title race. They didn't quite make it . . . but their new manager made it clear that they would be giving it their best shot again, when kick off time came around.

HOPES ARE DASHED

Liverpool's hopes of retaining their League-championship crown flickered and died over the first week-end in May, as they lost two matches while Arsenal, already ahead on points and goal difference, claimed the prize without even needing to win their last two games. A 4–2 defeat by Chelsea at Stamford Bridge, just hours before Arsenal drew at Sunderland, left Liverpool needing to win against Nottingham Forest at the City Ground to have even a hope of halting the Gunners' inexorable charge . . . and when Liverpool were beaten 2–1, it meant that Arsenal were already champions, even before they met (and beat) Manchester United at Highbury.

So, despite having had two points deducted after their Old Trafford fracas with Manchester United, the Gunners were clear winners of the title they had snatched in such dramatic fashion at Anfield two seasons previously, when the race went to the final seconds of the final game. This time, Arsenal had 77 points, with two games to go, while Liverpool remained on 73 points, with only Tottenham Hotspur to meet at Anfield . . . which meant, of course, that even a win over Spurs wouldn't enable them to catch the Gunners.

For Graeme Souness, it was a disappointing way to end the season, so soon after his installation as manager – the more so, as Liverpool's first two games under his direction had produced resounding victories

and revived hopes of a last-ditch charge to the championship. But while Liverpool's manager acknowledged Arsenal's quality –"I do believe that the team who win the title are the best in the country" – he also summed up: "I'd say that, over the season, Liverpool have lost the championship, rather than Arsenal having won it."

After the defeat by Forest, he declared: "I've been disappointed at certain things I've seen during the games since I took over as manager – on this occasion, for instance, we made defensive mistakes that cost us the game. I don't believe anyone can be delighted at losing the championship . . . what I really want to know is how much it is hurting my players. I would like to think that any team of mine, now or in the future, will be hurting badly on an occasion like this."

But if the season ended on a sad note, there was also a declaration of faith about the future. Like this: "I know the burden I must carry – to be compared with all my predecessors in the Liverpool manager's chair. I accepted that when I took the job on. My target for next season? – To maintain the high standards Liverpool have set over the years, to get hold of some players . . . and go on to win the First Division."

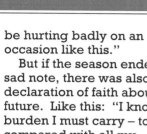 **Below:** John Barnes hurdles over the outstretched legs of Tottenham's Gary Mabbutt during Liverpool's 2–0 victory in their final League game of the '90–'91 season.

...RESULTS...

Football League, 4 May

Chelsea 4	Liverpool 2
Kerry Dixon (2)	*David Speedie*
Dennis Wise (pen)	*Ronny Rosenthal*
Gordon Durie	

Football League, 6 May

Nottingham Forest 2	Liverpool 1
Nigel Clough (pen)	*Jan Molby (pen)*
Ian Woan	

Football League, 11 May

Liverpool 2	Tottenham Hotspur 0
Ian Rush	
David Speedie	

Final League Position

	P	W	D	L	F	A	Pts	Position
Liverpool	38	23	7	8	77	40	76	Second

If Liverpool failed to retain the championship of the Barclays League at the end of season 1990 - 91, they had the certain satisfaction of picking up a consolation prize . . . because, by finishing as runners-up to Arsenal, they qualified for entry into the UEFA Cup. And the UEFA decision to lift the ban imposed on Liverpool after the Heysel-stadium disaster of 1985 meant that the Anfield Reds could look forward to season 1991– 92 with double anticipation.

Not only would they be playing in European football again, but they would be celebrating their centenary, as well, as they followed Manchester United and Aston Villa back into the European arena. . .an arena which Liverpool had graced for no fewer than 21 consecutive years, up to Heysel. Liverpool, indeed had staged English football's logest running show in European tournaments, between 1964 and 1985, as they competed in every single one of the competitions open to them.

Their first European match had been against the Icelandic part-timers of Reykjavic, on August 17, 1964 - a match they won, 5-0, with Gordon Wallace having the honour of being their first marksman in Europe. That season they went to the semi-finals, and a year later they were the losing finalists in the Cup-winners Cup. They competed again in the European Cup, the Fairs Cup and, in season 1972 – 73, the UEFA Cup, becoming the successors to Tottenham Hotspur, whom they had knocked out in the semi-finals.

Cup – winners Supreme

Then it was the Cup-winners Cup, and another UEFA Cup success in season 1975-76, followed by the supreme prize - the European Cup - in season 1976–77.

Liverpool retained the trophy in 1978, won it again in seasons 1980-81 and 1983-84, and then came that disastrous day in the spring of 1985, when Heysel claimed the lives of football fans as Liverpool prepared to take on Juventus.

Liverpool had reached the final with a victory over Panathinaikos in Greece, and their last marksman was Mark Lawrenson, because in the final, Juventus scored the only goal - though, in view of the pre-match events, the result was immaterial.

By the time their European safari had been temporarily ended, in 1985, Liverpool had played no fewer than 140 matches, with this proud record of results: WON 84, DRAWN 26, LOST 30.

Liverpool's squad of 1984 with the European Cup, which they had won for the fourth time.

Goals scored - 282; Goals conceded - 105. They played their 100th match in Europe against Dinamo Tbilisi at Anfield in September, 1979, and lost on home ground only three times - against Ferencvaros, Leeds United and Red Star Belgrade. And only Ferencvaros and Red Star beat them home and away.

The European Cup had been won four times, the UEFA Cup twice, and along the way Liverpool had scored 11 goals against Dundalk, from the Irish League, and the Finns of Palloseura. Graeme Souness and Terry McDermott had hit hat-tricks in the same game (against Oulu), and Souness had scored three times also against CSKA Sofia. Other hat-trick marksmen in the European glory days had been: Alun Evans (Bayern Munich), John Toshack (Hibernian), Jimmy Case (Slask Wroclaw), John Wark (Lech Poznan) and Ian Rush (Benfica).